The Prodigal Son

By Elvin Colon

Copyright © 2009 by Elvin Colon

The Prodigal Son
by Elvin Colon

Printed in the United States of America

ISBN 978-1-60791-982-7

Unless otherwise indicated, Bible quotations are taken from The Authorized King James Version.

www.xulonpress.com

Forward

By Elvin Colon

Because I have been so blessed, I'd like to share these blessings with you, the reader of this book. I believe that everything that occurred in my life, including my addiction to heroin, was meant to be used by God to make me the man I am today. In my heart, I hold very dearly the mothers, fathers, siblings and friends who have a child or other loved one still lost in the Hell that is drug addiction. My purpose in writing my story is to give these people hope regardless of how grim the situation may seem. No matter who you are – racial/ethnic background, economic class, gender or degree of education – addiction is cruel and ruthless; an equal opportunity destroyer. For several years, I've felt called by God to let those who love a drug addict know that there *is* hope! For me and thousands of other addicts, that hope, was through the saving grace of Jesus Christ. My mother endured seemingly endless and sleepless nights knowing that I was living on the mean streets of North Philly; she knew there was nothing she could do for me except to pray continuously for my safety – and she did! My faith assures me that her prayers on my behalf stirred God's heart, and that He blessed her with my recovery. My recovery from drug addiction was enough for my mother, but God has taken *me* on a much wider mission. The Bible tells me that "the vessel in the potter's hand is marred, and He made it another." I was marred and flawed, yet God came into my life and made me into a new person. This is truly a miracle! I now know that God truly loves me, and what makes this so essential in my life is that He has given me the ability to love Him back! No longer will I take Jesus for granted; I want to follow His ways and He has become the center of my life.

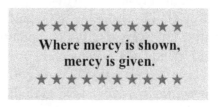

★ ★ ★ ★ ★ ★ ★ ★ ★ ★ ★
**Where mercy is shown,
mercy is given.**
★ ★ ★ ★ ★ ★ ★ ★ ★ ★ ★

Jesus Christ is *everything* to me. He had mercy upon me, and I know He has just as much mercy for the parents, family members, and friends of the addicted.

In my journey to recovery, I learned that if I acknowledge the power and mercy of Jesus, He will love you as you've never been loved before! Often, in the depth of my addiction, I felt like an animal; something that was no longer human. I believed I would be addicted for the rest of my life. I know my mother loved me even during this dark period in my life. But sometimes we can become so angry at our addicted loved ones, and become convinced that they will never change; we put them out of our lives for good so we don't have to think about them – out of sight, out of mind.

I am convinced that this is not what God wants for the addict or for his/her loved ones. This is what "the Enemy," whom Christians call Satan, wants for us all. Specifically, Satan whispers to us that we shouldn't pray because God doesn't hear or answer our prayers. We addicts are lost causes and cannot change. Those who love us should know that we are always going to be this way – lost and addicted forever. Now I know that these are lies taught to us by Satan, the father of all lies. Satan doesn't want us to know and believe that God loves us and doesn't want us to stray from His Word. Satan wants us to believe that, in our addiction, we have gone too far and cannot be forgiven, much less helped. Another lie! In my experience, I believe that this is one reason why addicts continue to destroy their bodies and their spirits; they believe these lies, as do their families and friends.

During my years of addiction, I gave God no reason to love me and help me, but He did anyway because this is what God does; He doesn't need to have a reason to love me. Long before I was born, God sent his Son to die on the cross to wash clean the sins of mankind for all eternity. All I had to do was to claim that freely-given gift. But as an addict, I never gave God the chance to help and love me.

My God, who answers prayer and does not scorn the petitions of the humblest of your servants, do not despise my prayer because you know me to be a sinner, but let my cry come to you.

--Book of Common Prayer

Somewhere very deep in my heart, I thought that God loved me, and yet I continued to believe Satan's lies day after day, week after week, and before I knew it, 22 years had completely passed me by. I don't want this to happen to you! If you're an addict, please start praying *today.* There's no "right" way to pray; just talk to God as you would talk to anyone else; it's that simple. He understands you and loves you regardless of things you've done that you may not be proud of; God already knows these things anyway, so just talk to him. Ask God to take away your urge to use drugs and your obsessive thoughts about using drugs. He did this for me! No, it didn't happen overnight, but it *did* happen. Tell God that even though you don't understand his Word and what's happening in your life, you want Him to be a priority in your life from this day forward and ask Him to show you the way to freedom from addiction.

Something you must understand is that God often works through other people; He will send people into your life to help you overcome your addiction. Don't reject their help! In fact, if you choose to recover from addiction, many people will come into your life; how can you tell if these people from God? Think on this: God will never send anyone into your life who will interfere in your recovery from addiction. He will be the one who is directing you out of the horror of addiction! For example, this book that you hold in your hands was sent to you for a reason, not by accident. Albert Einstein said that coincidence is God's way of remaining anonymous. You're reading this book because God sent it to you! He doesn't care, at this point, how you became addicted, but he does want to help you see your way out of this trap. The word "angel" in Greek means "messenger of God." Let these messengers help you find your way out of Satan's darkness.

To those who love an addict, I know that the horror of addiction is just as hard for you as it is for the addict. I know that at this time it feels as if the situation is hopeless. This book is also for *you,* to give you hope in your Moments of despair. Jesus Christ already paid the price for all of our sins; won't you accept his salvation *now?* Put aside your despair, anger, and guilt about your loved one's addiction; these feelings won't help you, but God will.

Finally, a sincere message for all those who are addicted and holding this book: please understand and believe that you are *not* hopeless and beyond help. All you have to do is let go of all the things that are keeping you mired in your addiction and accept God's free gift of a renewed life simply by saying, "Lord Jesus, would you please help me? I know I can't get out of this black hole by myself and I'm tired of being alone. Please show me your love and give me the wisdom to accept it." If my story gives you hope beyond your addiction, it will give me great joy. If you need a friend who wants to listen and help you, I would be so happy if you'd contact me at elvcoll@comcast.net. My greatest hope is that everyone who reads this book, whether you are an addict or someone who loves an addict, will find recovery as I did: through Jesus Christ, my true Lord and Savior.

This book is dedicated to my Mom, whose love and prayers gave me so much, and to Anthony, who will never be forgotten.

★ ★ ★ ★ ★ ★ ★ ★ ★ ★
As for me and my house,
we will serve the Lord.
—Joshua 24:15
★ ★ ★ ★ ★ ★ ★ ★ ★ ★

Elvin Colon
2009

Table of Contents

Note:U Readers should be aware that this book contains some sexual references; please use discretion. Some names are pseudonyms for confidentiality purposes. Unless stated otherwise, text containing facts about drug and alcohol effects and addiction were written by Margaret R. Kohut, Master Addiction Counselor, exclusively for this book.

The Parable of the Prodigal Son

(From the Holy Bible, Luke 15: 11-32)

Acertain man had two sons. And the younger of them said to his father, "Father, give me the portion of goods that falleth to me. And the man divided unto them his living. Not many days after, the younger son gathered all together and took his journey into a far country, and there wasted his substance with riotous living.

And when he had spent all, there arose a might family in that land; he began to be in want. He went and joined himself to a citizen of that country who sent him into his fields to feed swine. And he would fain have filled his belly with the husks that the swine did eat, and no man gave unto him. When he came to himself he said, "How many hired servants of my father's will have bread enough to spare, and I shall perish with hunger! I will arise and go to my father and will say unto him, "Father, I have sinner against heaven and before thee, and am no more worthy to be called thy son. Make me as one of thy hired servants."

He arose and came to his father. But when he was yet a great way off, his father saw him and had compassion, and ran and fell on his neck and kissed him. The son said, "Father, I have sinned against heaven and in thy sight and am no more worthy to be called thy son." But the father said to his servants, "Bring forth the best robe and put it on him, and put a ring on his hand and shoes on his feet. Bring hither the fatted calf and kill it; let us eat and be merry. For my son was dead, and is alive again. He was lost and is found. And they began to be merry.

Now his elder son was in the field; as he came and drew nigh to the house, he heard music and dancing. He called one of the servants and asked what these things meant. The servant said unto him, "Thy brother is come and thy father has killed the fatted calf because he hath received him safe and sound.

He was angry and would not go in; therefore, came his father out and entreated him. And in answering said to his father, "Lo, these many years do I serve thee, neither transgressed I at any time thy commandments. Yet thou never gavest me a kid that I might make merry with my friends. But as soon as this, thy son, was come which hath devoured thy living with harlots, thou hast killed for him the fatted calf."

And the father sayeth unto him, "Son, thou art ever with me, and all that I have is thine. It was well that we should make merry and be glad. For this, thy brother, was dead, and is alive again. He was lost, and now is found."

Chapter One

In the Beginning

"Welcome, children, from the other side. In the darkness, your eyes are open wide. And if you listen while the streets glisten, here's where our story begins." (Savatage – "Streets: A Rock Opera")

Charles Dickens began his novel of a boy growing into manhood, *David Copperfield,* "To begin my life with the beginning of my life, I record that I was born." Since I too am writing this book of a young man's struggle with the spiritually poisonous things in life, I record that I was born in 1964 in Bristol, Pennsylvania. My mother and father were both born in Puerto Rico; they came to America in the 1950's to begin a new life in the land of prosperity they had heard so much about. My family was a large one: I have six brothers and four sisters. My younger brother is the "baby" of the family, and I'm only ten months his senior. Mom was pregnant for nine straight years, and with all the children to care for, Mom was a busy lady!

It's interesting to note that my grandfather died from complications of alcoholism before I was even born. My father, too, was a heavy drinker; his doctor told him that if he didn't stop drinking he too would die. Dad stopped drinking in 1970 when he was in his 40's. As I recall, he just stopped. No treatment program, no 12-Step program, nothing. He made it look easy. I'm not certain, but I wonder if somehow I filed this away in the back of my memory and then years later when I was addicted, envisioned that stopping would be that easy for me. If so, this was a truly fatal vision since drugs had long since killed my spirit. Both my mother and father are still living and have been married for 55 years. Mom never drank or did any kind of drugs. I've heard that some medical researchers believe that alcohol and other kinds of drug abuse may be an inherited condition of some sort, like a birth defect or a faulty gene somewhere in a person's genetic makeup. If some people have this inherited or genetic condition, drinking heavily and doing a lot of drugs may make them more likely to become seriously addicted. Others say that drinking and drugging is *learned* behavior; that is, we learn it from the environment in which we grow up. This could explain why there is so much alcohol and other drug abuse in poor, minority communities. I'm no scientist and certainly don't know the answer to this mystery. Neither does anyone else, I think. At least, not yet. Maybe someday we will know, and this will save a lot of human misery in this world. All I can tell you is what happened to me and let you draw your own conclusions.

We were brought up in the Catholic Church and taught to fear God, but I remember attending a Baptist church from age ten to age fourteen, so I had a variety of religious experiences as a child. A bus would pick up me, my sisters and my brothers on Sunday mornings and drive us to church. My mother used the time we were away from the house to catch up on chores. My father was working. That's not to say that Mom did not reinforce what we learned in Sunday school; she reminded us every day about our faith in God and following the Ten Commandments.

One Wednesday night a neighbor invited me over to his house for a Bible study group that his mom was hosting. There was a guy there playing a guitar and singing and I was instantly enchanted! I started attending the group study regularly and also brought my younger brother with me sometimes. It was then that I remember first having a relationship with Jesus Christ. Though my years, problems and travels took me far away from my relationship with Christ, the memory of those nights and the Christian fellowship with people, the Bible studies and the music is a great part of what pulled me back and saved my life.

Growing up in my family wasn't easy because my parents didn't have any difficulty disciplining us when our behavior or attitudes needed to be corrected. Mom was the main disciplinarian in our home; whether this had anything to do with Dad's heavy drinking, I don't know. What I do know is that both my parents worked very hard all the time, both in and out of the home, to make sure there was always a meal on the stove for us to come home to and clean, decent clothes to wear. Being one of the only Puerto Rican families in our small town was challenging at times. We tried our best to fit in and did not let others know that our parents were "right from the island." We didn't want to be seen as different from the other kids. In our home we spoke mostly Spanish but on the streets and at school we only spoke English.

When I went through puberty, I began to develop a very low sense of self-esteem. No one ever told me about "the birds and the bees;" around other kids my age, I had to pretend to know things about girls, love and sex that I really didn't know. As a result, I didn't feel at all comfortable around girls. I became terribly self-critical because I had a rather "chubby" look. I suppose no young boy or girl is satisfied with the way he/she looks; we always find the slightest fault or flaw and turn it into a big deal! I recall looking at an ad in a magazine that had a picture of Charles Atlas, the famous body builder, and wishing desperately that I would grow up to look like him. Today I imagine the young boys are looking at pictures of Arnold Schwarzenegger – a seven-time Mr. Olympia winner – the same way. Never mind becoming a world-famous movie star and then governor of California; all young boys see (and maybe girls too) are all those muscles! When I told Mom that I liked a girl when I was in the fifth grade, she slapped me in the face, telling me that I was still wet behind the ears as far as girls were concerned and that I was forbidden to even think about girls at my young age. I felt a lot of resentment about this, thinking that I wasn't allowed to do things that other boys did. Mom let it be known that she thought American girls were "trouble." So, as a matter of fact, were American boys; all bad influences that I must stay away from. Needless to say, she didn't like any of my school and neighborhood friends if they were American. Looking back, I can see that I had slowly started rebelling against Mom's rules. I know she was only trying to protect me from the wild, bad world out there, and she did the very best that she knew how.

Our parents were strict because they felt they had to be. Coming from Puerto Rico, they were careful about letting us get involved with what American children were doing that they thought could be destructive to us. I remember one day after school when I was very young - maybe four or five - my eldest sister, Esther, was dropped off in front of the house by a boy in a car. My father saw her from the window and before she could reach the house he met her outside and gave her a beating right there on the spot. It was unusual for my sister to be in trouble; she was the one who always did the right thing and made my parents proud. She helped them with reading and writing and things they needed to do that they could not do themselves because of their limited educations and lack of fluency in English. My Dad only had a third-grade education and my Mom, though she graduated from high school, came from a school background in Puerto Rico that was quite different from American schools. Esther's beating took place during a time when my father was drinking, and it was shortly after that when he stopped.

When we, the kids, were young, we weren't allowed to have friends visit our house, and with ten siblings we learned to entertain each other. I was really close to my brothers and sisters when we were young. As they reached their teen years my older brothers were often in trouble, going out with their friends, drinking and doing drugs. I used to watch how it would upset my mother and I remember thinking at some point, when my brothers John and Martin would come home high or drunk, that I would never do that to my Mom. I would tell them, "You're not doing right, you're bad and upsetting Mommy." They, naturally, told me to shut up; nobody listens to little brothers! They assured me that when I got older I would do the same things that they were doing. I denied it and I swore I never would. As we all got older and spent more time away from the house with friends from school, we eventually grew apart. Each of us took different paths in life and we became more distant as the years went by. By the time I was four-teen two of my older brothers had already moved out of our parents' house. John had an apartment with his girlfriend and they had a baby. Martin moved in with a different friend every month, only coming home long enough to ask my parents for money.

My sister Janis, who was just a year older than I, walked home from school one day with a boy from the neighborhood. Janis, like Esther, was a good kid, never in trouble and did well with her studies. But my Mom was hard on the girls, very strict with them;

she saw Janis from a distance coming down the sidewalk and went out of the house to meet her. She disciplined Janis in front of the entire neighborhood and all the kids walking down the street on their way home from school. My Mom gave Janis a beating that I would never forget. That night Janis ran away from home. She went to stay with my brother John for a few weeks, but later went from one friend's house to another. I have never seen Janis since that incident and this is a significant loss in my life.

Chapter Two

__Anthony__

"Do you remember? Look at me and all the things we said we'd be. We'd beat the house, we'd push the odds. But somehow, in reaching for the stars I think we went a bit too far." (Savatage – "Streets: A Rock Opera.")

Anthony was my best friend. We met when we were in the seventh grade. I think the thing that drew me close to him was that he was very different from me in a lot of ways; we were brought up differently and yet we had an instant liking for each other when we met. I was brought up in a strict Puerto Rican home; my Mom was especially strict when it came to obeying her, doing well in school, not being obsessed with the mysterious allure of teenage girls, and never, ever, doing drugs or drinking alcohol. However, Anthony's parents were not like this: he was more of a "free spirit" than I was and I thought that was great! I had very low self-esteem and Anthony didn't. He was able to talk to girls without making a fool of himself. And he had a great sense of humor; he could always make me laugh even when I was down about something. Anthony didn't take himself too seriously and allowed himself to grow without becoming nervous and uptight.

Since I wasn't allowed to have friends over to our house after school or on weekends, Anthony's mother, father, brothers and sisters always welcomed me into their home and treated me almost like their own family member. I felt good when I was with Anthony and his family. He knew a lot about rock music; I found this to be so cool! I was taking guitar lessons at the time, and Anthony really liked this about me. He asked his parents to buy him a guitar; he taught himself to play without ever taking a lesson; I marveled at this special gift that he had. Anthony even *looked* like a rock star, with handsome blonde hair and blue eyes that made him very attractive to girls. He had an air of being very sure of himself – something I completely lacked. I wanted to be just like him, but I knew I never could be.

There I was – so shy with girls, with my dark Hispanic coloring, not as good in school as Anthony was, and without his easy and accepting family. He was fair-haired and had a quick, easy smile. I wanted to be like him, not like *myself*. He was always honest with me about everything. I trusted him; he was someone I could count on. Both of us always knew what the other was up to, what was going on in our lives, and we shared our problems and also our hopes and dreams in the future. Like most boys our age, we had dreams of starting a band together and being rock stars – such aspiring "guitar heroes" we were! Although I couldn't play a note, Anthony had natural talent playing the guitar. I marveled at how he could hear a song on the radio and just like that, he could play it.

Anthony and I did everything together; we were inseparable. He had a smaller physical build than I did, so we complimented each other in that way. Besides, I think he liked knowing that if we ever had to defend ourselves in a fight, I would be there for him in any situation. With Anthony, I always felt like I "fit in" with everyone else, despite my poor self-esteem and lack of confidence.

FACT: All drugs, including alcohol, cause a condition called "disinhibition." This is a state where the user's judgment is seriously impaired. The user may do or say things that he/she would not normally do because of inhibitions created by morality and laws. Disinhibition is responsible for a great many bar fights, domestic assaults, and even homicides. However, voluntary intoxication is never a viable defense in court cases.

Like most teenagers during this time period, Anthony and I experimented with drugs. In fact, the first time I smoked marijuana and drank beer was with Anthony and a girl we knew. I recalled how my mother felt about drugs, but when they passed the joint to me I thought I'd better take it or they might think I wasn't cool. Again, I just wanted to fit in. I was so uptight about everything in my life; I felt as if I constantly had to be careful about anything I did because I feared getting into trouble with Mom. I was afraid of her punishment, and mostly, her disapproval. I was caught in between my life as a teenager and my life as my mother's son. When I was with Anthony I felt free of fear and disapproval because Anthony wasn't that sort of friend. He was always showing me how to avoid becoming wrapped up in my own life and taking myself so seriously that life as a teenager just wasn't fun for me as it should have been. I was trying to grow up, to become a man, and to live and enjoy my life without harming others in any way.

> When I was a child, I spoke as a child, I understood as a child. But when I became a man, I put away childish things.
>
> — 1st Corinthians 13: 11

Anthony made me a promise that our drug use would not go beyond drinking beer and/or smoking marijuana. He wasn't into "hard drugs," and neither was I at that time. But I discovered that no matter how good your intentions, substance abuse *always* leads to trouble. Sure enough, trouble found me and my life changed completely in a matter of moments.

One day Anthony, Larry (another friend) and I were riding around smoking pot and getting high when we heard that someone in a nearby back yard wanted to fight Larry because of something he'd said. Being high, none of us were likely to have been thinking straight. Larry went into the yard to confront the person who wanted to fight him; Anthony and I wisely stayed in the car, finishing our joint and not really wanting anything to do with fighting. But, with our impaired judgment, we decided to go into the back yard where Larry and the other guy were still arguing back and forth, "posturing" like tough guys. It all seemed silly and pointless to me, so I said, "Will somebody please hit somebody and get this over with?" The guy who wanted to fight Larry told me to "shut the fuck up." So I hauled off and hit him and he fell to the ground. Then things turned very ugly. The guy I'd hit picked up a baseball bat as he was getting up and started to come after me, Larry and Anthony. Seeing the bat, and feeling our pursuer's rage and determination to get at us, we all tried to get out of the yard through a very small gateway; this was the only means of escape available to us. The next thing I remember is that the guy wielding the bat, Larry, and I were in the front yard. Our would-be attacker dropped the bat and ran from the scene. Larry and I instantly began looking for Anthony; looking back through the gate, we saw Anthony lying on the ground having horrible convulsions. The emotions that ran through our minds were a blur, but I remember Larry carrying Anthony into a nearby house, but it was not the house of anyone we knew; we were in a stranger's living room. I picked up the phone and called 911. Anthony went into a coma and died three months later from massive injuries caused by the guy with the bat – a death meant for me, but suffered by Anthony instead. My life would never be the same.

I felt emotionally numb after Anthony died. When he died, I started to die inside. I missed him every single day; nothing was the same without him. I believed that he died because I was acting like a bully by challenging "somebody to hit somebody." Well, that's exactly what happened and because of my big mouth and trying to act tough, my best friend was dead. I had no idea that my best friend would die because I was high on marijuana and wanted to show off how tough I was. Did I set Anthony's death in motion? I think that if I had told Mom how agonized and guilty I felt, she may have reminded me of Jesus' assurance that *"greater love has no one than this, that he would lay down his life for his friends."* I suppose that through the years I have forgiven myself, but the truth is the truth and I must tell only the truth in this book.

I blamed myself for Anthony's death, and so did his family. The guy who actually killed Anthony was never found, but even if he had been, I would still bear the guilt of his death. He was the best friend I've ever known. Sometimes I wonder how our lives would have progressed if we could just go back and re-do that one horrible day. I truly believe that Anthony's death played a major part in how my own life took a terrible downward turn from this point. I certainly felt far from God's love and forgiveness at the time. I gave up on myself. I began to succumb to evil influences that wreaked havoc in my life for many years to come. This much I know is true: Anthony was the best friend anyone could ever ask for, and to this day I still miss him.

Chapter Three

My Early Drug Experiences

"Listen to me from deep down inside; I'm the madness that just will not die. With no regrets of what I'll do to you." (Savatage – "Streets: A Rock Opera.")

After Anthony's death, I set out upon a course of self-destruction. I had no personal knowledge or understanding of God's plan for my life or of Jesus, our Savior. I did know that Jesus forgave his own murderers from the cross but I had no idea that this kind of forgiveness had anything to do with me. This agony seemed to be with me every day; I killed my best friend. How could I ever be forgiven and cleansed of my grief and remorse?

Since I was without the knowledge of Jesus and wandering in the darkness of my own soul, like many people in my situation I looked for something outside myself or God: I turned to drugs. I learned that drugs can change your mood. When I was sad or angry, I

> ★ ★ ★ ★ ★ ★ ★ ★ ★ ★
> **The biggest troublemaker you'll ever see is the one looking back at you in the mirror.**
>
> —Midwestern Proverb
> ★ ★ ★ ★ ★ ★ ★ ★ ★ ★

could use a drug to change these unbearable moods. It was easy! I didn't have to think or feel, or even care about anything. I only had to put a chemical into my body and all my pain about Anthony's death would disappear for an hour or two before it came crashing down upon me again.

In school, I was a very good student until the ninth grade when I started smoking marijuana and drinking alcohol. I stopped caring about school then – it was no longer important in my life except as a place where I could meet up with my friends and get high. Instead I became the "class clown" and was always an annoying distraction to teachers and other students. With little else to do with my time, and wanting to seem "cool," I started selling pot at school and cutting classes.

By the time I was old enough to work, it seemed like I was never able to keep a job because of drugs; my use of pot and alcohol was more important to me than working and learning how to make an honest living. My Dad supervised a car wash for forty years, and he would always let me work there, but I always managed to screw that up, too, by not getting up for work in the mornings and even stealing things out of the cars. Dad would always give me another chance, but I ruined every one of those chances. This became the pattern of my life; chances given, and chances thrown away. Much later in life, I learned that God, through His son Jesus Christ, is a God of endless chances. When people give up on those who keep ruining all their chances for changing their lives, God *never* gives up, and never turns them away when they seek Him in prayer. If only I had known and understood this when I was a child, maybe my life would have turned out very differently.

During this time I began smoking marijuana very heavily. This, I discovered, was a cool drug. Its effects on me depended upon my mood at the time. Mostly it's a depressant drug (a "downer") but it also has some hallucinogenic effects. I smoked marijuana when I was feeling anxious and needed to calm down, to "chill out." When I was upset about something, instead of working the problem out I smoked pot. Instead of managing my anger, I smoked pot. When I wanted to fit in with the crowd, I smoked pot. In fact, I smoked pot just because I liked it; I didn't even need a reason. Most drug researchers agree that marijuana isn't physically addictive, but that it does have a powerful psychological/emotional addiction potential. I can attest that this is true.

I learned something else about marijuana; it was even better when I drank a lot of alcohol with it. Since alcohol is also a depressant drug, using the two drugs together really gave me the oblivion I needed and wanted. Beer, wine, whiskey; who cared? I knew that, unlike marijuana, alcohol was seriously addictive but I didn't care. It wouldn't happen to me, so why worry about it? I didn't. I just drank.

I thought I was really smart back then, but what I didn't know is that the kind of heavy marijuana use that I was doing causes an ***amotivational syndrome.*** I'm now aware that teenage pot smokers can develop this condition, causing them to be disinterested in school or any kind of learning. It's not the same as the brain damage that alcohol causes; I didn't care if I learned anything or not. I didn't think about my educational needs for my future (if I even had one). I wasn't motivated to learn and now I believe I understand why: Not only was I devastated with grief and self-blame about Anthony's death, but I wrongly chose to cover up those horrible feelings by smoking marijuana heavily.

FACT: Methamphetamine is the most dangerous drug in America today. Made from extremely toxic chemicals by "meth cooks," it is powerfully addictive and causes extreme damage to all bodily systems and organs, including the condition known as "meth mouth" where teeth and dental tissues are destroyed. Addiction follows quickly after first use, and of all the illegal drugs in the US, meth has the highest relapse rate. Chronic meth use is eventually fatal, usually from overdose.

When I was sixteen, I met my first real love when my brother introduced me to methamphetamine. He taught me how to use a needle to shoot this killer drug into my veins when I turned seventeen, and how I loved the feeling! This is an "upper" drug usually called "speed." I knew nothing about how horribly destructive and addictive meth was; I only knew that I loved the feeling of energy and intoxication it gave me. The high lasted longer and was much more intense than anything I had ever experienced before. I liked it and I did not care that there was a big, wide world out there filled with wonderful opportunities. I was high! I had a great potential for success in life, but I didn't know it. I was just into feeling good at that moment. Jesus Christ loved me, forgave me, and died for me and I didn't understand or accept it. The saying goes, "Once you get your first meth high, you can kiss your future good-bye." I was there!

It was about this time that I left my parents' home and I have not returned to live with them since. Instead, I moved in with a friend; we did nothing all that summer but use and sell meth and throw "keg parties" with lots of beer. In fact, I don't think I got much sleep during the entire summer! High on meth, mellowed with alcohol; this is how I spent all my time. My brother was dealing speed and when other people found out that I had access to a lot of it, suddenly I had a whole new group of "friends."

Among them was Donna, the girl whom I thought would be with me forever. She liked drugs and sex as much as I did, and being older than me, she had more experience in both. Donna made me feel wonderful! She taught me things you don't learn in classrooms. She made me feel good about myself. Or, perhaps it was the drugs. This relationship was doomed from the start; I was sick, she was sick......we were incredibly toxic with each other. But try to tell this to a seventeen-year-old drug user who was getting laid two or three times a day! Even then, I was going nowhere fast, and so was this relationship. Donna had her own apartment; who cared that she had no gas or electric in the house! Our entire relationship was based upon sex and drugs. It was an "off again, on again" relationship; she constantly cheated on me and this hurt me a lot. I got used to it – I didn't know any better than feeling hurt and betrayed by someone I loved. When our toxic relationship finally ended, I believe that I then set out to hurt women in general before they could hurt me. I only used them for drugs, money or sex. I didn't trust women because one day I came home and found Donna in bed with another guy. She rarely acted as if I was important to her, like I should always understand her every mood and whim. In the end I had to accept that I wasn't what Donna wanted. I think that in every relationship one person loves more than the other. Of course, the more life hurt me, the more drugs I did to try to simply not feel the emotional pain. Now I know that without Jesus in my life, I did the only things I knew to keep living and putting one foot in front of the other. I didn't even know how to treat another person at all, much less a woman. I either used them or fell in love with them the first time I met them. It was a dim, dismal, soulless life, but it was all I had. And it was only an introduction to the living Hell that would soon engulf me.

Chapter Four

<u>Heroin – Meeting the Devil</u>

"Who am I foolin' – I'm the king of the ruins but I'm doin' well tonight. I've got dreams to sell tonight. Ghost in the ruins, burnin' like gasoline. See the runaway there on the corner? Somebody's daughter had a pretty face so somebody bought her." (Savatage – "Streets: A Rock Opera.")

My life had become one night after another night of smoking pot and shooting speed, but the meth wasn't doing anything for me anymore because of my increased tolerance to the drug; it took more and more to achieve the same effect. I needed something else. Something more powerful and more relief from the sheer pain I felt in my day to day life. Meth wasn't the answer for me anymore. I saw my friend Rick shooting something into his arm that wasn't speed. I asked him what it was and if I could have some. **This was a defining moment in my life** when Satan entered my soul and remained in control of me for many, many years. Only Jesus Christ could save me, but I did not know this. I was Satan's pawn. In later years, after my salvation, I learned that Jesus Christ and the Devil were in a battle for my soul. At this particular time, Satan was winning. My Lord's victorious healing would only come many years later.

On this particular night, Rick gave me ten units of heroin; the first thing I did was vomit. This is because opiate drugs like heroin trigger the nausea center in the brain. I didn't care, though, I loved the feeling the drug gave me instantly. It was like nothing I've ever done before and I knew I wanted to do it again. Of course, I had no idea what I was in for! Somehow, deep inside, I knew that by shooting heroin, I crossed a line into a world from which I could not return. Most of my friends never crossed that line; every drug was okay except for heroin. It didn't matter to my drug addict friends whether I smoked heroin (called "chasing the dragon") or shot up with it. It seemed to me that shooting heroin had the fastest effect because my blood in my veins carried it directly to my brain. When I shot up that first time, I didn't know just how much force the drug had. I didn't know I would become heroin's slave.

What is there to say about heroin addiction that hasn't already been said by thousands of people from Hollywood celebrities to politicians to "regular" Moms and Dads in your own neighborhood? Heroin addiction is enslavement, pure and simple. When you're hooked on this drug, it owns your life. Using

> "Well, I smoked a lot of grass and I popped a lot of pills. But I never met nothin' that my soul, it could kill. May God damn the pusher man.
>
> —Steppenwolf
> "The Pusher"

it is unbearable, and not using it is just as unbearable. This devil is known on the streets by many names: Captain Jack, smack, snow, blow, poppy, and others. But for me it was one of the Horsemen of the Apocalypse whose name was Death. (Book of Revelation). The opium poppy, grown in parts of China, Thailand, and Cambodia, is a beautiful flower, yet its seed pods literally eat away your mind. Opium is the best pain killer known to mankind at this point, and this was intended to be its primary purpose; to ease the suffering of those in terrible physical pain. Like anything else in life, opium has a down-side; it produces extreme euphoric effects – the ultimate "feel good" drug. Its addiction power is almost insurmountable. Heroin is a derivative of opium just like codeine and morphine. It is an illegal drug in the United States because of its horrific addiction potential. Once heroin owns you, it owns you forever. Heroin street dealers know this, and yet they continue to sell their poison to young and/or desperate people like me. But I will not judge the street dealers; they must answer to a greater power than I.

Within two months, I was shooting up every day; Satan had claimed what was his. I never thought I would be a junkie using any needles I could find – those I found on the street, bent needles, dirty needles, using the same needles that other addicts had just used. I used dirty puddle water to mix with the heroin. By this time, my goal was getting high 24 hours a day. My job was to get the money any way I could to achieve this goal. I had no real home at this time; I slept wherever I could find a place to sleep, even if it meant sleeping in the woods behind the McDonald's.

As a juvenile, I had a breaking and entering charge on my record. I broke into a friend's house because I knew he was at school and that nobody was home. I stole $100 in cash so I could get high. I was finding out that it took a lot of money to be a heroin addict. When I was in my friend's house, stealing his money, I had a moment of clear thinking: What was I doing, stealing from a friend? Something was whispering inside me, telling me that this was wrong, but I couldn't stop. I needed my dope, and that was the most important thing right then. It was as if my spirit didn't want me to do these things, but my body and my obsession with heroin were stronger.

Today I understand what happened to me that day; I know that my spirit was calling out to Jesus, who was much stronger than my body's irresistible quest for heroin. Looking back to these days when I didn't know Jesus as my Lord and Savior, I wish I had understood that without Jesus, I am nothing. I didn't know that Jesus could take away my desire for

> "Come out of the man, thou unclean spirit." And Jesus asked him "What is thy name?" He answered "My name is Legion, for we are many." The unclean spirits were cast out and went into the swine.

heroin. I could be healed and saved, someone who was special to Jesus as we all are, for his love has no limits.

I quit school in the 10th grade. All I wanted was to get high, so why waste my time getting an education? How foolish was this prodigal son, wasting my body and my mind? Since I now know Jesus, I got my GED and am taking courses to become a Christian counselor. But before I reached that point in my life, things would get a lot worse before they got better.

Chapter Five

Paying the Price

"These streets glitter in the dark. Don't sleep! Red eyes, sunken and dark, dream deep. These streets never sleep....still, never wake." (Savatage – "Streets: A Rock Opera")

If you're an addict, as I was, or if someone you know and love is an addict, then you know that addiction comes at a very high price. I'm not only talking about the ever-increasing money it takes to buy drugs, but this lifestyle carries its own price. Loneliness, fear, shame, and obsession this lifestyle is pure agony. There's nothing safe or worthwhile about it; you are nobody, you have no future, and you live only for your next shot. The suicide rate is high among chronic addicts because they feel hopeless about their lives. If this agony – this darkness – is all there is why torture yourself by continuing to live?

I've been looking back on my life and all the things I've done today.
I'm still searching for an answer; I'm still looking for the way.
But the wreckage of my past is still haunting me —
It just won't leave me alone.
I still find it all a mystery – could it be a dream?
The road to nowhere leads to me.

—Ozzy Osbourne
"The Road to Nowhere"

Once you set foot onto that road to nowhere, Satan demands that you pay the price. Only Jesus Christ can redeem you from this price of damnation. After all the things I did to my body, I can't help but wonder sometimes why I'm still alive. Today I believe that Jesus redeemed my then-worthless life because he loved me and He has work for me to do in this world.

When I was working in a car wash in Trenton (NJ) I was doing both heroin and crack cocaine. It was dark by the time I headed home. Suddenly I was jumped by fifteen young black men. It seemed that they didn't want to rob me (as if I had anything!), just beat me up. I had crack and a pipe in my pocket and they didn't even discover it. I heard one of them say "Get that white boy!" This puzzled me because I am 100% Hispanic. Perhaps they were just looking for someone to assault, and I looked white to them.

Broken and bleeding, I managed to get away from them and ran to a corner store for help. A man gave me a ride to the bridge and then I walked the five miles to my parents' house. As I walked, I smoked the crack that was in my pocket. Something was wrong with me, though. And it was something serious, something different than just being drugged up on crack and heroin. As I lay down and tried to understand what was wrong, I thought I might have a concussion. I was scared now, and called an ambulance. At the hospital I had an MRI done; it turned out that I had two broken vertebrae in my neck. The doctor looked at my medical record and was simply amazed that I wasn't paralyzed from the neck down. After being beaten so badly and walking five miles to get home, he said it was a miracle that I could move at all.

A miracle? Yes, it was. Even then, Jesus was looking out for me. I didn't know Him, but He knew me. "I knew you in the womb," He said. I believe that Jesus saved my miserable life that night because He had a destiny for me that didn't include drugs, stealing, and paying Satan's price. He wanted me to tell the story of how His undying love healed me from heroin addiction and that He will do the same for anyone who calls to Him.

When you're just beginning to pay the price for your addiction, it's easy to fall into self-pity as I did. This is a *choice* we make. Making the choice to remain miserable and addicted surely generates self-pity. Thomas Merton wrote that "Despair is the absolute extreme of self-love. It is reached when a man *deliberately* turns his back on all help from anyone else in order to taste the rotten luxury of knowing himself to be lost." After all my experience as an addict and paying the heavy price of my addiction, I believe that being lost in self-pity is the opposite of having faith.

In speaking of Jesus Christ, the prophet Isaiah wrote, "Come unto Him, all ye that labor. Come unto Him ye that are heavy laden and He shall give you rest." At this point in my life I badly needed the rest of the comfort found only in Jesus. I had survived Anthony's death, using unclean needles to shoot up with, and being beaten so badly I shouldn't even be alive. I didn't realize that I've been living for the wrong reason – to get high – not that I had no reason to live. Everyone has pain in their lives; choosing self-pity is optional!

The worst price of addiction that Satan commands is a lack of knowledge of Jesus Christ as your personal Lord and Savior. Matthew wrote in his gospel that Jesus said, "Whoever acknowledges me before men, I will acknowledge him before My Father in heaven. But whoever disowns me before men, I will disown him before my Father in heaven." It wasn't that I intentionally disowned Jesus; I didn't even know of Him and his promise of deliverance.

My life was going to change yet again. I would have a chance of recovering from my addiction, or I could deny that chance because of the pull of the drug. A turning point in my life was just around the corner.

> **Captain Jack will get you high tonight –**
> **And take you to your special island.**
> **Captain Jack will get you by tonight –**
> **Just a little push – and you'll be smiling.**
>
> — **Billy Joel**
> **"Captain Jack"**

Chapter Six

In and Out of Rehab

"You call me when you're weak; for me you'll lie and cheat. You'll never get away – with me, you're here to stay." (Savatage – "Streets: A Rock Opera.")

By now, I was beginning to think that "maybe" I had a drug problem. What a revelation! I was in the Intensive Care Unit for a week after I was jumped and my neck was broken; I was immobilized and sedated most of the time. I was moved to a regular room for several more weeks. For me it was like the equivalent of detoxification. I couldn't wait to get out of the hospital so I could get high again.

In 1982 I checked myself into rehab at the suggestion of my family and friends who claimed to be worried about me after my scare with the broken vertebrae and hospitalization. My brothers took me to a place secluded in the mountains of Pennsylvania. I was there for a day when someone handed me a

51

FACT: Numerous studies have shown that 12-Step programs like Alcoholics Anonymous and Narcotics Anonymous have only about a 2% long-term success rate. In-patient programs, while more successful, still have a high relapse rate, especially among heroin addicts.

toothbrush and told me to clean the bathroom. I asked for the nearest phone; I called my brothers and told them what they asked me to do. They were at the door to pick me up in just a few hours with a case of beer and an ounce of pot. So much for my first rehab.

The cycle of more drug use and abuse continued until 1988 when I was taken by my brothers to Eugenia Rehab in Lafayette Hills. They kept me for a month then sent me to a rehab community in Williamsport, PA where I was part of a "recovery town." It was five hours from where I lived; I think everyone's hope was that if I got away from my drug peer group, I would have a chance to really get clean – and take it seriously this time. But the issue was that I simply took my problems right along with me. This is called a "geographical escape," and addicts do it all the time. We think that if we get far enough away from where we did drugs, we could start all over. But life, especially addiction, doesn't have a rewind button. There are no "do overs" when we really make a terrible mistake. No matter where you go, there you are. I *was* the problem; heroin was only a symptom of the messed-up person that I was, the person who didn't know the healing power and love of Jesus Christ.

I admit that I wasn't very serious about rehab. In fact, I thought it was a big joke. I went to rehab for all the wrong reasons – mostly I wanted my family to think that I was ready to stop using drugs. The truth is that in my heart, I couldn't wait to get out and get high again. I thought it was good that I had 28 days to cleanse my body of drugs so I could start all over again and not have the high tolerance that I had when I went into treatment. I'd be able to get high on a lower dose – or so I thought. I now know that our bodies "remember" our tolerance level and return right back to it when we start using drugs again.

Something I did learn in rehab was that when people first start using, they enjoy the high caused by the drug. But as time goes by and you become an addict, you *need* the drug in order to feel normal, meaning that you won't feel heroin's horrible withdrawal symptoms like intense body aches, extreme anxiety, chills and fever and a non-stop craving for the drug. Believe me, all the awful things you've heard about withdrawal from opiates like heroin, morphine and codeine (to name a few) are absolutely true. Withdrawal from these drugs isn't fatal, but sometimes you wish it was just so it would be over.

I usually got high again the same day I left rehab. I couldn't hold a job, and I didn't really want to. Since I had no education, all I got were minimum wage jobs. Besides, working interfered with my drug use. I thought that life was one big party that never ended; my only goal in life was to stay high.

I couldn't live with my family anymore because they were tired of me stealing from them. Anything that wasn't nailed down, I would steal from my Mom or my sister to buy drugs. God's commandment to "honor thy mother and father" was lost on me. I knew what I was doing was wrong, but again the drugs won me over. Even my brothers who introduced me to speed thought that I was way over the edge with my drug use. I felt all alone in life, with no one to turn to. How I wish I had known that with Jesus, we're never alone! With Jesus, there are no "last chances." If I had given up on myself, perhaps my family had given up on me too. Through it all, though, I believe in my mother's steadfast love.

From 1988 until 1990, I must have stayed off dope for a total of six months. After a failed relationship I went back to Philly to get high again, and I stayed that way. I had nowhere to live but my car, and my addiction got even worse very quickly. I went to yet another rehab; they sent me to the Salvation Army's long-term rehab center. I stayed there about six months, and it was then that I met Diana, who I believed was the girl of my dreams! The counselors told me that I was not far enough into recovery to have a serious relationship, and that I needed to focus only upon my sobriety. I didn't believe them, of course. After knowing her for six months, we were married.

Only a short time after my marriage, I started doing dope again. Even though I was a newlywed, my life never felt complete without shooting up. I'm certain this is the reason why I never lasted very long in recovery; a piece of me – the piece that wanted to get high and stay high – was missing and I couldn't

---

Last Chance For Salvation?

One of the thieves who was crucified with him said "If thou be Christ, save thyself and us. But the other rebuked him saying," Dost thou not fear God? We receive due rewards for our deeds, but this man has done nothing amiss." And he said unto Jesus, "Lord, remember me when thou comest into thy kingdom." And Jesus said unto him, "Verily I say to thee that this day thou shalt be with me in paradise."

—Luke 23:39-43

---

live the straight life. In addition to using drugs, I also started to gamble on sports. On one occasion I lost $11,000 in five hours of betting on a single Sunday afternoon. What I didn't know is that drug use and serious sports betting often go hand-in-hand. Drugs make us feel like we're on top of the world, that we can't go wrong. When we lose money, we have to "chase our losses" by betting even more to make up for what we've lost. Losing so much money in one day scared me, and my drug use escalated.

I stole money from Diana and spent all of it. This was the turning point in our short-lived marriage. She said she'd had enough, she was through with me. Diana was seven months pregnant at the time when she kicked me out of her life. Oh sure, I cried....crocodile tears because I could no longer use and abuse her for money to feed my drug habit. I didn't even feel human anymore; I felt thoroughly evil, and cared for no one but myself. I didn't even think about my unborn child. I sank so low that when Diana left me and went to live with her sister, I would sneak into their apartment at night to sleep; I would wake up early, steal all their valuables, and leave before they found me. These abominable actions continued for about a week, until there was nothing left for me to steal. On the last day, as I was sneaking out the front door with a TV – the only thing left in the apartment, there was a note on the inside of the door saying, "Elvin, it's a girl." I glanced at the note and kept right on moving; it never registered on me that I was now a father with responsibilities for his daughter. Instead, I sold the TV and bought more dope. I recall thinking that the longer I lived; the more I wanted to get high. For the first five years of her life, I didn't even know my own child and never paid a penny for her needs. Deep within the dark place that was my soul, I think I must have felt some guilt about this but not enough to do anything about it – like getting clean.

I lived on the streets for the next four years other than a night or two every now and again in a homeless shelter or a short stint in yet another rehab. I did not shower, I did not change my clothes, and I did not brush my teeth. I hung out at a store near where Diana worked in a check cashing place. I would see her occasionally. She came to me one day on the street to tell me our daughter was in the hospital and was having problems with her heart. She invited me to go to the hospital to see Kaycee. I went, but I could not get close enough to hold her. Seeing her and being so emotionally distant from her confirmed in my mind that I did not even deserve to know her. In hindsight

I believe that this was Diana's way to see if she could pull me out of the life I had chosen and bring me back from this fate worse than death. But the attempt failed; the next time I saw Diana was when she found me on the streets to ask me to sign the divorce papers. I remember feeling very sad as I signed, but making sure she did not see that her giving up on me and our marriage mattered at all. But it did matter.

If all of this sounds like I had sunk as low as it's possible for one human being to go, it wasn't. In the early 14th century, Dante Alighieri, an Italian poet, wrote his masterpiece, *The Divine Comedy*. The first part of the work is called *Inferno* – Italian for "Hell." It tells the story of Dante's visionary journey through the nine circles, or levels, of Hell. Each circle is more horrific than the one before it, reserved for certain kinds of unrepentant sinners who denied God, His commandments, and His Son, Jesus Christ. Each sinner is punished eternally in a manner that fits their crime against God and mankind, God's beloved creation. As Dante enters the gates of Hell, he sees a sign which says, *"Abandon all hope, ye who enter here."* Circle by circle, Dante is led through the ever-present agonies suffered by the truly and forever damned. Finally, Dante reaches the ninth circle, reserved for malicious liars who bore false witness for their own gain, treacherous murderers, and betrayers. In the center of this circle is Satan himself, bound in ice for having committed treachery against God; in his mouth, eternally ripped and torn by Satan's fangs, is Judas Iscariot, the betrayer of Christ.

In the *Inferno,* Dante escapes from Hell. I did not. I remained in the ninth circle – a betrayer of God's will and of His Son, Jesus Christ. I cared only for my own gain. I lied and stole from my friends, my family, and even from my wife to get what I needed – drugs. I betrayed and abandoned my daughter.

I didn't even have a soul to sell.

> Abandon all hope, ye who enter here

Chapter Seven

Life in the Badlands

"I never wanted to know, never wanted to see. I wasted my time until time wasted me. So I plot and I plan, I hope and I scheme for the lure of the night and an unfinished dream. I'm holding on tight to a world gone astray as they charge me for years I can't pay." (Savatage – "Streets: A Rock Opera.")

So began four years when I lived on the mean streets of north Philly, surviving on discarded metal and a few handouts from preachers. Having nowhere else to go, I began living in abandoned factories. They were filthy, rat-infested, unsafe, and full of people like me and some people in even worse shape than I was; they might have killed me just to steal my dope for the night. We called this the "Badlands" and they lived up to their name. I didn't ask too many stupid questions, like why and how I was still alive. I didn't want to know the answers. I just put one foot in front of the other every day and went hunting my dope. Each day I sank lower and lower into Dante's vision of Hell. Despite all this degradation, I felt that I belonged here. The only people I had anything to do with (I can't call them friends since this term had no meaning there) were other homeless junkies; they were the only creatures that wanted anything to do with me. "Just get the fix" was everyone's prime directive.

> "No, you can't get too low when you're so damn high. Time to roll again on the blessed Hellride."
> — Black Label Society
> "The Blessed Hellride"

Jesus said, "I was naked and you clothed me. I was hungry and you fed me. I was in prison and you visited me. Whenever you have done these things for the least of my servants, you have done them to me." But the love of Jesus seemed very, very far away in the Badlands. Like Dante's eternally damned souls, those who entered there abandoned not only all hope, but also even the slightest thought that things might ever be different. Jesus? A myth rammed into kids' heads to make them behave. A nice story with no basis in the harsh reality of the Badlands. Nope, no Jesus on the mean streets of north Philly.

To make a few bucks to buy my dope for the day I pushed around a shopping cart and picked up scrap metal like copper, aluminum and others that had a monetary value. I had a nice scam going: I would jump the junkyard fences at night and steal the metal I sold the junk guy that day to sell again. I'm lucky I never got caught at this since it could have cost me my life. I think they did catch onto me at some point because one night while sifting through the metal I was shot at. On the streets, the summers are hot and the winters are brutally cold in Philly. I pushed that shopping cart through feet of snow while feeling desperately sick because I hadn't had my shot yet. I often slept in the scrap yards that I was stealing from, having nowhere else to go.

I carried a little pouch that held my "works," meaning my needle and spoon to cook the dope before shooting up. I lived like an animal, eating out of garbage cans, drinking out of open hydrants or half-drunk discarded bottles of soda left with the trash on the sidewalks. It was very dangerous to walk the streets of the Badlands at night; other junkies would rob me of my drugs, many times at gunpoint. As I gained "street smarts" I learned to hide my dope up my rectum so no one – not junkies or cops – would find it. I had guns put to my head more times than I can even remember, and I was actually shot at twice. A lot of the junkies wanted to hang out with me because I was big and could carry more scrap metal and push a heavier cart. One afternoon after scrapping all day with another junkie on the street we rolled up to the scrap yard and sold our load. When we got paid the woman scrapping with me wanted her half to go get her drugs. I didn't want to give it to her. I worked hard for that money and she hardly did anything. When I turned to walk away, she picked up an empty bottle and cracked me over the head with it. I think she expected me to fall to the ground but when I didn't she ran. I had a headache for the night and a little bleeding that left a scar but nothing a fix wouldn't take care of.

> "A gut-wrenching fever – addicted to death
> You don't give a fuck if it means your last breath.
> There's no reasoning why, but the mirror don't lie –
> You're a junkie."
> — Ozzy Osbourne
> "Junkie"

One day I found a mattress in the garbage. I pulled it out and moved it with my cart to the bridge under I-95 near Bridesburg. I set myself up with the mattress, some scrap blankets and a place to heat up my dope. A street junkie's paradise! I remember lying there one night under the bridge when it was raining and thinking I really had it made; I wasn't going to get wet under the bridge. I laid my head down for the night. As the storm rolled in and the rain got harder the water rolling off of I-95 started pouring down over the mattress and splashing me in the face. I was too drug dumb to get up and move the mattress. I remember lying their hoping I would die before I woke.

The next morning I opened my eyes and the sun was shining on my face. It should have been a sign of hope, but my only thought was that I had to get going to make some money by scrapping to get my fix for the day. A streetwise entrepreneur, I also made money by hanging around watching for cops for the dope dealers selling their stuff on the corners. I'd get about one fix for five hours of being a look-out.

I wasn't making enough money being a look-out and selling scrap metal and I knew of only one way to get the money I needed. I began to prostitute myself to other men. As unbelievable as it sounds, I learned about doing this at Narcotics Anonymous meetings listening to all the other junkies tell stories of their addicted lives on the streets that never sleep. When I smoked my first joint at age fourteen, if someone had told me I'd be a heroin addict selling sex for money I would have laughed. I'm not laughing now when I see young people like I was degrading their bodies to buy drugs. Does anyone know where the love of God goes when you do unimaginable things to your body late at night when the streets are most dangerous and you're jonesing (craving) for your fix? Is there anything you *won't* do?

One day I ran into a junkie who had stolen a car. He needed a fix but had no money. It had been a few years since I had been to see my parents and I knew if I could get there I could get them to give me some cash. I told him if he gave me a ride to Morrisville I would get him some money for a fix. He drove me to my Mom's home. My Dad was in the yard. He hollered to my Mom inside, "Look who's here!" My Mom came to the door and she started screaming, not in joy but in terror. My hair was long and scraggly, my clothes were dirty and disgusting, and my appearance upset her terribly because I must have looked like the street junkie that I was. She was crying and holding her chest. My Dad quickly came to help. He did not want my mother upset. He asked me to leave and he gave me $40.00 just to get out of there and away from my mother. I got what I came for and I left. The next day my mother sent two of my brothers to find me. They walked the streets of north Philly looking for people pushing shopping carts. They asked around and found someone who knew me and where I might be scrapping that day.

Later my brother told me he had given the guy $5.00 to tell him where to find me. I was surprised because my brother never gave me a dime. They took me to the Salvation Army and they made sure I was off the streets before they left and went home to report to my Mom. I stayed there about three days before checking myself out.

I know this sounds odd, but sometimes it felt like I was waiting for something and I'd no idea what it was. It wasn't the old junkie denial routine of "I'll quit when this or that happens." It wasn't even about quitting; it was just about *waiting.* I don't know if this "whatever it was" was good or bad, but I knew I was doing more than just wasting time until time wasted me. Sometimes I could almost catch a glimpse of these ghosts of my own destiny before they vanished into my drug-induced stupor.

One day I went to a church I had seen and I thought it might be a good place to beg for money and maybe get some kind of help. I was desperate for both. I went on a Sunday morning; I was in disgusting shape. I'd been living on the streets for two years without a bath or change of clothes or even a tooth-brushing. I spoke to the church pastor and talked him into giving me a meal, a shower and ten bucks – enough for a fix. Never one to shun a good scam, I went back the next week. The pastor invited me inside the church to talk about getting me some help. Then he asked me how much I would charge to let him give me oral sex. I wasn't even surprised; nothing surprised me anymore. I was "dope sick" in deep withdrawal. All I could think of was the money, so I said it would cost him forty bucks. Well, when he was done he gave me the money. Boldly, I asked this "man of God" to give me a ride to a place where I could buy drugs. He did, and I shot up the dope right there in the back seat of his car.

After this I kept going back to him day in and day out. He got what he wanted and I got what I craved. It was a fair arrangement between a junkie and a morally dead so-called pastor. It suited us both. In my mind I never associated this pastor with God, nor did I ever blame God for the ruin of my life. After a time, though, it began to dawn on me that perhaps he shouldn't be doing this. I also felt a twinge of shame that I was using him for what he could give me. We had a savage co-dependency on each other; I was addicted to heroin and he was addicted to me and the sex I gave him. Worse, he stole money from his church and parishioners and gave it to me in exchange for sex. He continued to take me to buy drugs and I kept on shooting up right in front of his face. Then I would go sleep on the streets and do this sick dance with this sick man all over again the following day. We even agreed upon scheduled days and times when he would find me on the streets, or I would call him to come and get me.

> "Against the Holy Trinity shall fight the Accursed Three: The Devil, the Anti-Christ and the False Prophet or Corrupt Man of God, for he is not."
>
> — Writer Unknown from the Dead Sea Scrolls

This pastor began to say that he wanted us to stop because it was becoming too expensive for him. Oh no ya don't! I held our arrangement over his head, telling him that if he didn't keep giving me money for drugs, I would tell his church what was happening. Because of my threats he had to borrow money for me. I was using about $200 per day for heroin, and $100 per day for crack cocaine. I drained this man dry, exhausting all his financial resources including thousands of dollars worth of collectable, expensive Lionel trains that he sold to get drug money for me. We were both lost, stumbling blindly in the darkness of a damned soul. Finally, after two years, his parishioners somehow found out that he was giving me stolen money every day and they stopped giving money to this church. He was quickly reassigned to another church.

Sometimes, today, I wonder how he's doing and if he has ever repented of his actions with me and has found the grace and forgiveness of God through Jesus Christ. There's a part of me, even today, that finds it hard to trust pastors and other people associated with church. This man graduated from the Princeton Seminary, so he was not under-educated in theology. He saw my condition (how could he miss it?) and took what he wanted from me. I was shooting heroin ten times a day and also smoking a lot of crack; I was not in my right mind, and still very young. I had a $200-per-day drug habit.

FACT: At least 90% of male and female prostitutes are drug-addicted. More than half of these are HIV and/or hepatitis-positive and will die within five years without treatment.

Could he not see the wrongfulness of his actions? I will not judge him or cast the first stone. But I will pray for him, that he will "go and sin no more" as Jesus declared to the woman caught in adultery. My own hands were unclean in those years of my life, not just this pastor's. When all the shouting, blaming, weeping and debating is over, every sinner has the free will to follow God's law or turn away from Him. Jesus stands at the door and knocks; we can choose to open that door or bolt it shut.

Then, a crisis: My cash flow was gone I needed to find a way to get the money to keep my addiction satisfied. I was sick from withdrawal symptoms. It was March 29th, 1997 the day of my daughter's birth; she was three years old today. Half tempted to go to Diana for money, I ran into a man on the street trying to sell a bottle of pills. That seemed like a better idea at the time; I could take the pills and kill myself and it would be the end of my misery. I had no idea what the pills were but the junkie took what I had for them and I found a half finished bottle of soda in the trash.

I used it to swallow the pills and they were going down easy and fast. After about fifty pills, something inside me decided that this was a stupid idea and I made my way to Northeastern Hospital. I went to the emergency room and told them what I had just done. I was filthy and not sure if they moved me to the back quickly to work on me or to spare the other patients from having to look at me. I was put on a bed in the back. I remember the hospital being very busy that night and despite my drugged stupor I remember hearing the head ER nurse telling another nurse to move the "filthy drug addict" to the back so they did not have to look at me. They used charcoal and tubes to pump the drugs from my stomach. When I was stable, they sent me to another rehab. When I got out, the cycle began again. A year or more later I was broke and tired and did not have the money for drugs. I thought if I could check myself into another local rehab they would give me a fix for the night to help me feel better. I checked myself into what was going to be my last rehab. I just didn't know it yet.

Chapter Eight

Jesus Christ Becomes Lord of My Life!

"Gotta get back, gotta get back – I never meant to take it this far." (Savatage – "Streets: A Rock Opera.")

In 1998 I was in detox and rehab again, and the guy who worked at the admissions desk, Danny, was gay. I, of course, still had the thinking process of an addict and I saw him as someone from whom I could get money for drugs in return for sexual favors. When I got out of the clinic Danny offered to let me stay with him and I readily agreed. I saw him as someone I could manipulate; what I didn't know is that he viewed me in the same manner!

I continued to get high, but it wasn't quite the same this time. By December of 1998 I didn't see any hope that I could stop, yet something inside me really wanted to stop using heroin. I was steered to a methadone maintenance clinic as an outpatient. You see, methadone is a drug that doesn't take away your desire to use heroin, but it certainly reduces cravings for the drug; it's more like an "insurance policy." It's not as dangerous as heroin and its effects last longer. Methadone sometimes gets a "bad rap" because people don't understand how it works and how it must be taken properly. Why give more dope to a guy who's already a junkie?

I often wondered if I was gay, or maybe bisexual. I really didn't know who I was anymore, nor did I know the truth from a lie. Danny, who took me in off the streets, was gay and yes, I had sex with him. Doing gay prostitution on the streets definitely messed with my mind! I moved in with him because I thought I was gay. I tried to be what he wanted, but there was a part of my damaged spirit that was repulsed by having sex with a man. I desperately needed love in my life; was this it? No, I craved love that had nothing to do with sex with either men or women. For me, this didn't exist in the world I knew. But it wasn't long before I learned that there is such a love not of the world but in the everlasting word of God.

My first day at the clinic was 24 December, 1998; on Christmas day, I was completely clean from all drugs and alcohol for the first time in many years. I don't think I realized it then, but it seems that Jesus Christ and I have the same "birthday" even though neither of us was actually born on this date. I was still living with Danny, who was starting to have some serious feelings about me. I didn't feel the same way, and I had to tell him so. I was afraid to do so because I thought I would lose the only place I had to stay. I was finally off the streets and I really wanted to stay that way. The only drug I was using was the methadone and I looked at that as a prescription to help my sick mind stay away from the other drugs I had been using.

FACT: Methadone is a synthetic opiate drug that works like, and is as addictive as, any other opiate. It is commonly prescribed as a pain killer. In federally licensed drug treatment centers, methadone is given to heroin addicts because of its longer-lasting effects; it can be taken daily rather than many times a day. It also prevents withdrawal symptoms that invariably cause relapse. Many heroin addicts are maintained on methadone long-term to prevent relapses with heroin. Methadone does not produce the "high" that heroin causes; in fact, it blocks the brain from feeling any kind of euphoria if heroin is used with it. Methadone maintenance programs have high success rates with long-term heroin addicts.

I knew, deep down, that I was not gay; I only had sex with men for money to buy drugs. Now that I was clean, I didn't want to lie about my sexuality any more. Danny seemed to understand. He agreed to let me stay with him and our friendship grew closer and more meaningful; we could talk to each other about our hopes and aspirations. I told him about my family and he helped me to reconnect with my mother. I told her I was off the streets. One of my brothers helped me to get a job driving a truck for a leather company. Things were going well for me, but I still felt that there was something missing in my life.

Danny and I also talked about our spirituality and I told him I would like to go to church. He had a friend who was always talking about her church and it was nearby. He contacted her and she promised to take me to church. I had a deep desire to go to church as I had when I was a child – before heroin trashed my life. I remembered how much I used to love church and knew that this was something I simply must do if I truly wanted to change my self-destructive lifestyle. I began to have hope that the desire to know Christ was still buried within me. I was afraid to show my degraded face in God's house; I didn't know what would happen. But I remembered that when I was very young and went to church with my family I felt close to Jesus and I had this feeling that everything was okay. I recalled feeling that Jesus never judged me; my heart felt uplifted.

"Hey there Lord, it's me. I wondered if you're free, or not asleep because this won't keep. Father, hear me – I am tired. Hold me closer, I am trying. Sweet Lord Jesus, heal my soul." (Savatage – "Streets: A Rock Opera" paraphrased.)

This wonderful girl took me to church with her in February, 1999. The moment I walked inside the church I yearned with all my heart to be close to God. The atmosphere at Saint James was warm and welcoming; people were casually dressed and genuinely friendly. The altar glowed from the sun shining through the stained glass windows and I could feel the warmth taking over my body. I felt good, I felt like I was home. We found a seat just as the two guitar players on the altar started to play. The song was "Lord I Lift Your Name on High" and the beat drew me in. I was immediately excited to be here and was already thinking about coming back week after week. The musicians were wonderful! Their sound took me back to a memory of the Wednesday night bible studies that I would attend at my friend's home as a child. The time came for the message from the pastor after the Gospel reading. Pastor Paul did not know me but I felt like every word he said was for my benefit. It was like he recognized me and what I was feeling. I had found my new church home and I was feeling like my recovery was really on the right track this time.

I wanted to know God, to love God, and to feel His love for me. I wanted Jesus Christ, who felt so far away when I was living on the mean streets of Philly as a junkie, to come into my life with all His healing power, salvation and forgiveness. I wanted *out* of the Dante's ninth circle of Hell. I called, and God answered. Jesus knocked, and I opened my door to Him. I didn't know quite what I was feeling, but I knew that the desire to use heroin again was completely gone from my body and my spirit. For the first time in twenty-two years, that destructive craving had left me. Jesus Christ became the Lord of my life and I knew that it would always be so.

I continued to be involved in the church, attending every Sunday for services and Wednesday nights for Bible studies. I joined a group taking a class to become a Stephen Minister, which is a lay person who does the work of God helping others when the pastor cannot be there. Stephen Ministers are a friendly ear and an encouraging voice to those in need. I knew I could be helpful, especially to people who were struggling with drugs and addiction. Since I told my story to the congregation, the truth was out there for everyone to hear and they thanked me for sharing my struggle with them. Many more people came to me for advice about their son, daughter, husband and more who was struggling with addiction. I had replaced my craving for drugs with a craving for the knowledge of the Word of God and Jesus Christ. I spent all my free time listening to Bible studies on the radio, and watching preachers on TV.

Several months went by and the duet of guitarists added a third guitar and player to their little band. In high school my brother and I used to sing in the school talent shows, though I did not have any formal training. I liked to sing and was confident I could hold my own. I asked them if they would allow me to sing with them. I had to endure an audition, which made me very nervous, but they liked what they heard. My talent was raw but they were willing to help me refine it. I began singing in the church band and attending practices during the week, making a joyful noise unto the Lord! My life was filled with activities around the Lord and I was so happy to be able to bring His word to people through music and my voice.

I started a new career and I was working for myself. Danny worked with someone who needed a cleaning person to care for their home. I said I would do it and that was the beginning of my own cleaning business. I cleaned their home twice a week. They had pets that I would walk and groom. They liked my work and referred me to their friends. The blessings were happening for me like a domino effect! The Lord was indeed working wonders in my life, as is promised for those who know and love Him, and heed His Word. The more He did for me the more I wanted to please Him, to know Him and to work for Him.

> **"Day by day, oh dear Lord, three things I pray. To see Thee more clearly, love Thee for dearly, and follow Thee more nearly...day by day"**
>
> **—From "Godspell"**

It may not be surprising to you that I didn't quite trust myself yet. My faith was new and I needed much time to grow in my relationship with Jesus Christ, compared to the long years when heroin ruled my life. I stayed on methadone in case I relapsed, but I discovered that as helpful as methadone could be for my bodily cravings for heroin, only God Himself could reach into my soul and snatch it from Satan's grasp. Only God could renew my spirit that was so desolate and starving for some kind of hope. In the Bible I read that if anyone is born again in Christ, they are new creations. Oh, how I wanted to be "new!" I remembered that God so loved the world that he gave us His only Son as the Lamb who takes away the sins of the world. ***Who, me?*** The junkie? The thief? The liar? The prostitute? The dope slave who abandoned his own child? Was it even possible that this thing that I became could be redeemed surely for some; it is too late, like Judas in Satan's eternal grasp?

I wasn't taking any chances, so I stayed on methadone. I struggled with my worthiness for redemption and with my fear of relapsing. Going to the clinic everyday was a hassle but it beat living on the streets looking for the next dollar for a fix. The clinic had a lot of rules and they required on-the-spot drug testing and screenings, blood work and physicals. If you screw up you were out of the program. It took years, ***many*** years of daily visits and weekly counseling and conversations with some good counselors, some great counselors and some still "green" counselors. I remember, near the end, thinking that I had more time clean and sober than some of the people I reported to. In time I was able to gradually stop taking methadone without a relapse; God, again, stayed with me through another difficult time in my life. I began to pull together the idea that the reason I never cared much for Alcoholics Anonymous or Narcotics Anonymous is because while they focused on a Higher Power or God *as we understood Him,* they don't speak about the power of having Jesus Christ in your life. AA and NA are open to all faiths or no faith at all, and for lots of people, that's just fine. But my healing came from God in Jesus Christ, my Lord and Savior, and none other.

Then Martha sayeth unto Jesus, "Lord, if thou hast been here, my brother would not have died. Yet even now I know that whatever thou wilt ask of God, God will giveth thee." Jesus sayeth unto her, "Thy brother shall rise again." Martha sayeth unto Jesus, "I know he will rise in the resurrection on the last day." Jesus sayeth unto her, "I am the resurrection and the life. He that believeth in me, though he were dead, yet shall he live. Believest thou this?" Martha sayeth unto him, "Yea Lord: I believe that thou art the Christ, the Son of God who has come into the world." And He said, "Father, I thank thee that thou hast heard me." And then he cried in a loud voice, "Lazarus, come forth!" And he that was dead came forth bound hand and foot with grave clothes. Jesus sayeth unto them, "Loose him, and let him go."

— John 11:21-44, paraphrased

Here is the record of Martha's unfaltering trust; here is the record of her hope, inspired by the teachings of Jesus Christ that *no one* is forever lost, even in death. For so long I felt that my spirit had long since died and my body would soon follow as mere dust in the wind. "Behold, I show you a mystery!" I have only a limited understanding of my God's omnipotent ways, but somehow my soul was as dead as Lazarus when Jesus Christ reached into my heart and said, "Elvin, come forth!" The stone in my spirit was rolled away, and I was let go from the bondage of drug addiction. This is my witness and my testimony to you, the reader. Believest thou this?

Chapter Nine

A New Wife, a New Life

GREAT ROAD SIGN!

"Tired of 12-Step programs?
Try the One-Step Jesus program!"

I continued to stay with Danny for about three years into my recovery; it was a way for me to build a solid foundation in Jesus Christ. From time to time he would want to be with me sexually, but as grateful as I was to him in many ways, I couldn't do that anymore. Gay prostitution was necessary for me to maintain my addiction on the streets, but those days were long gone and I would not be tempted merely to be kind to him. I had many sins upon my head – I was Legion – but I would never willfully engage in the sin of gay sex again because it is not of God. I don't judge Danny or any other gay person but I had drawn a line with my behavior and as long as I wanted God's gift of having

Jesus in my life, I would not cross that line, now or ever. Danny and I even talked with my pastor to make it clear that I wasn't gay and never have been. I once read a quote by Pulitzer Prize-winning author Toni Morrison: "You did the best you knew how at the time. When you knew better, you did better."

One of the things I longed to do better was to have a relationship with my daughter, the one that I had walked away from several years ago. I contacted Diana and asked to see our daughter, Kaycee. She hesitated at first, only allowing short supervised visits, for which I was grateful. I made attempts to rekindle a relationship with Diana, but she rejected my efforts and understandably so. She had no reason to trust me or believe in me after the cold, careless way I treated her when we were married. I learned that sometimes relationships just can't be repaired because our feelings, mostly our hurt and pain, remain in our hearts. We can forgive those who hurt us, but this doesn't mean that the relationship can pick up where it left off. Kaycee never knew that dark side of me; she was four years old before I met her. She was beautiful and precious, but she was afraid of me. She didn't know who I was – this strange man who suddenly walked into her life. I had a deep resolve that this was something I could, and would, change. Unlike when I was drugged all the time, I wanted my child to know me as her father who loved her completely.

It's true that I had trouble relating to women, so why should being a father to a daughter be any different? My disastrous first marriage with Diana certainly proved that, even though it gave me the gift of my precious daughter. After Jesus delivered me forever from drug addiction I honestly didn't have much desire for a new relationship. I wondered about this until I realized that all the desires of my heart, everything I could ever wish for was fulfilled by Jesus Christ in my life. I didn't need drugs *or* sex of any kind. Jesus had filled my cup to the brim and I was very willing to wait until He showed me the woman who was to be my lifelong companion. One extremely good thing about having "my cup running over" was that there is no room left for dissatisfaction, envy, lust, obsession or any other evil thing that came directly from Satan who, I'm sure, wanted me back in his enslavement. The very last thing that the angel who rebelled against God wanted was for God to heal my soul and claim me again, depriving the lord of Hell of his plaything.

When, in time, I expressed some yearnings to date again, Danny said that if I did, I would have to leave. In his mind, even though we were no longer together sexually, I was still his "partner." For me he was a business partner but for him, it was much more. We had moved into a new house with the mortgage in his name since I had no credit, but I paid the down

> "This above all: To thine own self be true. Then it follows, as night follows day, thou canst not be false to any man."
>
> — W. Shakespeare
> "Hamlet"

payment with money I had earned working as a truck driver. I was working hard, making an honest living to contribute to making the home comfortable for both of us. However, I was more concerned about building a relationship with my daughter and my Lord. While Danny said he understood, his actions said something very different. I didn't know what to do. I had put my life in Christ's hands. In the past the decisions I made weren't very smart, to say the least! I used to think that Jesus couldn't handle things a whole lot better than I could and this pride certainly came before my fall. I wish I could say that I had never made the same mistake twice, but just one look at my life shows this to be false. This time I *wasn't* going to make the same mistake. This time Jesus was going to be the shot-caller in my life, not me.

Sure enough, one day in church I saw a young lady named Laura who caught my attention. I was afraid to speak to her at first but after several weeks of saying hello and catching each other's eye

I approached her and asked her out for coffee. On our first date I told her everything about me, even about Danny. I didn't leave anything out, no matter how badly it sounded for me. I didn't plan to do this and maybe it wasn't a smart move, but I was done with lying. I can't change my past, but I don't have to lie about it. I knew God had forgiven me and redeemed me through Jesus Christ; I need not lie to myself or anyone else. I had certainly lied to myself often enough, telling myself that I didn't care about my life as long as I could shoot up. I told myself that nothing would ever change. I lied to myself about lying to myself, and I believed me! It would have been very easy to lie to this wonderful young lady about my past; I could find a way to keep it all secret from her. Sure, I could lie to Laura and buy myself a one-way ticket back to Dante's ninth circle of Hell, reserved for liars and betrayers.

No. Jesus was in my heart now, and had led me to meet this woman. I didn't know Laura, but He did. He already knew what was going to happen when I told her all about me. If she rejected me, it would hurt. But I would at least know that this happened for a reason; we were put in each others' path to learn a valuable lesson of some kind. If I remained true to myself and to Jesus, I could not lie.

My life story couldn't have been easy or pleasant to hear. I know it scared her because it scared *me* to tell it! Later, she told me that when she got home that night she told her children not to worry, that she wouldn't be seeing me again. Who can blame her? "Hey kids, I just met this guy who's been a junkie, a thief, a liar, a betrayer and a gay prostitute! He's coming to our house tomorrow!" Yeah, great. I didn't know how she felt because she was always nice to my face when we saw each other in church. She tried to avoid my phone calls, but I persisted and she must have felt sorry for me because she agreed to a second date. She later told me that the only reason she did was to tell me directly that she wasn't interested in a serious relationship with me. She was coming out of a divorce and was working two jobs; she had three kids and certainly no time for a romance with anyone, much less with someone who had a very complicated past. Laura had every reason to believe that I was going to be more work than she had time for and she didn't want to go there. Despite her efforts to end it, I persisted in getting her to see me time and again. Our conversations were always good and productive; we actually seemed to help each other. I was listening to her and God knows I had plenty of experience with counselors of my own, so I felt like I could give her some sound advice. My renewed faith helped me to bring her faith to another level.

I knew Laura was meant for me. She set my heart on fire! I loved her bright spirit and her sense of humor. I told her that one day I would marry her, knowing that God had lain this firmly upon my heart. It took a while for her to let me into her life and fully believe me but slowly, putting her faith in Jesus, she began to trust me and believe that my life changes were serious and lasting.

Our courtship was seven years of learning about each other, and we were in no hurry. We struggled with good times and bad. Just as he said he would, Danny asked me to leave shortly after I met Laura. I was afraid to be alone and with no credit and little to my name, finding a place to go was hard. Laura could see I was scared to be out on my own and agreed to let me stay with her until I could find another place with a roommate. She was adamant that it could not be permanent. Laura was, at the time, a mother of three who was separated for four years. Her husband had cheated on her and left her for another woman. As a result, she had trust issues going into our relationship and knowing all she did about my past just compounded her caution. I moved most of my belongings into storage and brought the necessities to Laura's house. Weeks lead to a month. The time I should have been looking for an apartment I spent helping around Laura's house and adding to my workload with new referrals for my growing cleaning business.

The time we were together was spent talking and getting to know more about each other. I worked hard to make her kids like me and perhaps convince their Mom we should stay together. On weekends my daughter Kaycee would come over and spend time with Laura, me and Laura's daughter Peyton. They are close in age and liked all the same activities.

Laura and I enjoyed doing things with the four kids. Each weekend it was something different.

We would go to the movies, bowling, roller skating. Anything and everything to make it an enjoyable time for all. We continued to go to church as a "family". The kids were enrolled in Sunday school and were growing in their faith. They too liked the music and the atmosphere at Saint James. As time went by Laura and I were sharing bills and were able to afford to make the weekends fun for our family outings. The idea of me moving out was no longer a frequent subject. I certainly didn't bring it up!

Laura's household was not like the one I grew up in. It was quite the opposite. Hers was the house in the neighborhood where everyone hung out. Her feeling was if the kids were there, she knew they were safe. There were no drugs, alcohol or guns for them to get into. It took a lot for me to get

> "I am my beloveds and my beloved is mine. Thou art beautiful, oh my love."
>
> — Song of Solomon 6: 3-4

accustomed to all this! Kids were in and out of the house all the time. Hanging out, watching TV, listening to music, playing games, eating all our food - I wasn't used to it though I said before I moved in that I would love it. I had ten brothers and sisters so a few neighborhood kids wouldn't bother me…but it did. Laura didn't care what I wanted; she wanted her kids where she could keep an eye on them. She did not want them hanging out on any corners, and the nearby park was littered with drug paraphernalia and broken beer bottles. It was often a subject of argument between us. Her response was always, "If you don't like it, leave!" It was her way or the highway, so I learned to deal!

In 2004 we decided it was time to move. Laura was in the same house she had when she was with her husband and it was now hers. Moving would make a new house a place we could call ours, and only ours. We spent months looking for a new home but nothing seemed to fit our wants and needs. We put her house up for sale and when it sold, we had to work harder to find a place to call home. During the search there was a bigger focus on our finances and a lot more stress in our relationship. We were arguing over every little thing. The day came when we needed to be out of the house. Not having any other options, Laura arranged for us to move into an apartment complex to rent month to month until we found a house. I wasn't helping with the choices because we weren't really talking. She had to make a decision for her family and she did that. Not happy that she signed a lease without me, I went out and signed a lease of my own on another apartment. The day we were supposed to be moving stuff to our new place we were moving stuff to our new places – plural. We agreed to go our separate ways. Laura said she was relieved; she was tired of having one more person to please. Her three kids were enough. The day she went to the closing for her house there was a problem with the loan for the person who was supposed to buy it. The sale fell through and she ended up moving back into her home a month later. For her it was an answer to her prayers. The kids hated their new apartment and missed their friends, so they were happy to help their Mom move them back *home.*

When we were apart, Laura worried about me. She would call and leave me messages because she just wanted to know that I was OK. She worried about me falling back into a self-destructive way of life. I would call and let her know I was fine. But she could hear it in my voice that I wasn't. It got harder and harder for me to talk to her. I would ask her to see me but she said it wouldn't be a good idea. She stopped going to the same church that I went to and looked for another church to attend. I turned to the pastor of Saint James for help. I asked him to talk to Laura for me. He agreed to see her but for her own sake and not as my messenger. He went to where she worked. It was a community center so visitors were not unusual. He asked for her to be paged and she came to the desk. She later told me she was so surprised to see him! Her relationships with him and with Jesus Christ were strong but she did not expect the pastor to come to her job. He asked her how she was, and she seemed fine but really just very tired. Tired of arguing, tired of worrying, tired of trying, and tired of being tired. He prayed with her before he left. He did not mention me to her at all, but he was sure she knew who had sent him.

A few days later Laura stopped by my apartment to check on me. I didn't answer the door right away and she was about to walk away to go back to her car, when I answered the door and called to her. She came back. I was in sweat pants and no shirt. I was lying down in the middle of the afternoon. I didn't do much of anything most days but lie around and think about everything. I wasn't reading my Bible anymore and I wasn't listening to Bible studies, I had stopped going to church meetings and practices for the band. My only connection to the church was Sundays when I would sing and leave. I did not want to answer questions from the congregation about where Laura was or why she was not in church.

I asked her to come in, half hoping she would say no because my place was not pleasant. She hadn't been inside before. She agreed to come in after hesitating, but said she couldn't stay long because she had to go pick up her daughter from work. I was embarrassed for her to see that I hadn't even unpacked a single box. I didn't have any furniture except a bed in the bedroom and a TV that was sitting on top of another unpacked box at the foot of my bed. I started showing her around - as if there was anything to see. My living room was a bunch of boxes I had taken out of the storage unit where I had been paying rent when I lived with her. On my bed was a disheveled blanket but no sheets and you could see the mattress. An ash tray overflowing with cigarettes was at the head of the bed, a habit she hated and was always trying to get me to quit. When I lived with her I never smoked inside the house, which cut down on the number of cigarettes I would have in a night. There wasn't really anywhere to sit down but the bed. It was obvious that I spent all my time alone lying in bed watching the TV. A pile of take-out containers was toppling my garbage. I could see it in her eyes she was disappointed. I had been there nearly two months and had not even attempted to make it comfortable. She didn't stay long.

When she left I crawled back into my bed and cried. The next day I woke with a new outlook. I prayed and I went back to listening to Bible studies on my way to work instead of Howard Stearn. I called Laura and thanked her for her visit. She had tears in her voice; she was afraid for me, worried I was slipping back to who I was before she knew me. She ended the call with "I'm praying for you" as I hung up I knew that I was going to be OK. I stopped feeling sorry for myself and instead of spending my nights alone in my apartment I went back to the church. I checked in with Laura more often and started coming by to help her with chores around the house and the yard. Five months later we were spending most of our free time together again.

The kids grew older and the eldest two graduated from high school and started college. They had jobs and were more helpful around the house. They spent their time out of the house more and more. I have to admit I miss the days of a crowded living room. Kaycee and Peyton turned into beautiful young ladies, their circle of friends broadened their time spent together was less and less. Kaycee stopped coming over as much because she wanted to spend her weekends at her friends' houses not her Dad's. Laura will tell you the "terrible twos" were nothing compared to the teen years! Kids want to be in charge of their own lives; they think they know what's best, and being with their parents is a fate worse than death to them. Inevitably this is the time when you will eventually hear your teenager tell you how much they "hate" you, a word that sends chills up your spine when it comes from the children you love. Church is suddenly not "cool" enough for them to bother with. You want to let them grow up, but at the same time you want to protect them. Laura had her hands full!

Having spent 22 years addicted and four of them living a true Hell makes it even harder for me to let the kids do what they want to do and go where they want to go. I don't want my daughter or Laura's kids, whom I have grown to love like my own, to experiment with drugs or even want them to drink a beer. In my eyes, the first one will lead to another and it will snowball into heroin before you know it. My biggest fear is that Kaycee will inherit my addictive personality. I know that this fear isn't rational, but no one ever said that love was rational, especially when it comes to your children.

Laura tried (and still tries) to coach me through some disappointments in my relationship with Kaycee; Sometimes I questioned her skills as a mother. She is more of a free spirit like Anthony's Mom was. I tend to be over-protective like my own parents were. Laura believes you can never be sure that what you are doing is the best thing for your kids; you just have to let them go and trust that God will take it from where you leave off. While I know she is right I still struggle with this even today.

In 2006, after five years of persistent asking, Laura finally agreed to marry me. She was officially divorced a year prior and we had grown closer every year that we were together. She said she couldn't picture herself with anyone else, so why not marry me? Laura wanted a small wedding, she said it wasn't appropriate to have a big wedding the second time around. I told her I wanted a big wedding because this is the first time I was marrying the right girl for the right reasons and it was going to be the last time I would get married. I can be a bit like a kid when I want my way, begging and begging until she caves in. She's a social junkie and loves a reason to get everyone together for a party so convincing her to have a big wedding wasn't hard. Our guest list grew and grew and we talked about all the people who had helped us through the years that we wanted to know we were together forever.

Because we met at the church during the contemporary service and many of the people in the congregation were important to us, we asked Pastor Paul if he would marry us during the Sunday morning service. He agreed that this would be the perfect time for us to re-affirm our faith in Jesus and each other.

Laura's son Jay was my best man and her daughter Genesis was her maid of honor. Kaycee and Peyton were bridesmaids. Our family and friends filled the church. The congregation had pulled out all the stops to make this day special for us. The pews were packed and the event was standing room only! I opened the service with a solo, "Amazing Love." I didn't get through the first line without crying. Every emotion from 44 years of my life came rushing back into my mind, my eyes and my voice. Luckily the band had anticipated this and they had a backup singer ready to sing the song for me. We followed up with the song "Made to Worship." As we sang I looked out over the crowd and my Mom and Dad were sitting up front. They were crying and I knew that this time my Mom's tears were tears of joy. Then it was time for Laura to come in. As she entered the

> "Set me as a seal on thine heart, as a seal upon thine arm, for love is stronger than death."
>
> — Song of Solomon 8:6

back door to come down the aisle with her father the room sounded like a Phillies playoff game not a church service! The beautiful smile on her face filled me up. She wasn't crying but she was beaming. Later she said that any doubts or concerns she had about getting married were drowned out by the applause. She felt God looking over us and Jesus' love filled her up. There was no more worry as she heard me singing to her when she came down the aisle the words of our special song:

Love Alone

No one would love me
If they knew all the things I hide
My words fall to the floor
As tears drip through the telephone line

And the hands I've seen raised to the sky
Not waving but drowning all this time
I'll try to build the ark that they need
To float to you upon the crystal sea

Give me your hand to hold
'Cause I can't stand to love alone
And love alone is not enough to hold us up
We've got to touch your robe
So swing your robe down low
Swing your robe down low

The prince of despair's been beaten
But the loser still fights
Death's on a long leash
Stealing my friends to the night

And everyone cries for the innocent
You say to love the guilty, too
And I'm surrounded by suffering and sickness
So I'm working tearing back the roof

And the pain of the world is a burden and
it's my cross to bear
And I stumble under all the weight
I know you're Simon standing there
And I know you're standing there

Words and music by Aaron Tate
Artist: Caedmon's Call
CD: Long Line of Leavers

Sometimes I still can't believe I'm married to this most precious jewel in my life, the "Pearl of Great Price" who has brought me so much joy in our seven years together that I can't truly express it. The very best thing about our marriage is that I don't have to hide anything from her. Deep in my heart, I feel no fear that Laura will find out something that I didn't tell her and our trust will be broken. My wife taught me the meaning of unconditional love and acceptance. Laura knows me inside and out! It wasn't easy at first because my track record with women wasn't spectacular and I thank God for her patience.

Sometimes I felt like cave man that was transported into the future and had to learn things about life and love beyond my understanding. Contrary to those funny TV commercials, marriage is *not* so easy that a cave man could do it! Knowing that God chose this woman for me from the beginning of time made it easier. I had the free choice to make a mess of another marriage if that's what I wanted. It wasn't. I can truly say that the words of Ruth sum up the spirit of our marriage:

> "Entreat me not to leave thee, nor to return from following after thee. For wither thou goest, I will go. And where thou lodges, I will lodge. Thy people shall be my people, and thy God, my God. And where thou diest, there will I die and there I will be buried. May the Lord do this to me and more if aught but death parts me and thee."

More than anything I wanted to be a husband to my wife and a father to my daughter and my wife's children. I searched God's Word for answers about what it means to be a husband and learned that a husband is the provider for the family and responsible for its protection and prosperity. Being a father is much more than a biological thing: It means being an active part of your children's lives, putting their welfare above your own, and teaching them how to live a Godly life, accepting Jesus as their Lord and Savior. Husbands and fathers lead by *example,* not by tyranny. I was ready to accept this challenge knowing that God would strengthen my resolve when I faltered and uphold me with His power.

Chapter Ten

Answering the Call: Becoming a Pastor

"Somewhere the sun shines, somewhere the light's kind, somewhere they seek the day."
(Savatage – "Streets: A Rock Opera.")

B ecause Laura had accepted me just as I was – past history and all – I decided it was time to tell my story in church. I was told that it helped many people, especially parents of addicts who had no hope for their lost children. I shudder to think about how many sleepless nights I caused for my mother and father, and by writing this book I want to reach out to these parents in their fear and grief.

For the past nine years I've been studying the Bible very intensely, and I can't seem to get enough of God's Word! So much stronger it is than any drug, and *what a high!* My soul was so starved that now I can't get enough of the spiritual nourishment of the Bible. It became my dream – and my calling – to become a pastor. I registered for college courses and am a third of the way through them. Five years ago I started a youth Bible study group at my home; it became so large that my pastor asked me to do the group in our church! Much to my delight, I became my church's youth minister. What a joy and a blessing it is to tell young people about the love of Jesus Christ and the miracles He will work in their lives! I have a lot of credibility with them because of my life history. They know I've traveled on all the streets where the dark hides all our sins to everyone but God. I've cheated both death and Satan many times through the power of Jesus Christ, and I believe my physical and spiritual survival makes an impact upon young people because I *did* survive only by the grace of God.

Sometimes, when I think upon all the responsibilities of being a pastor, I find strength in the words of John the Baptist, who, one might say, was the first pastor who proclaimed the coming of the kingdom of God.

"And all men mused in their hearts of John, whether he were the Christ or not. John answered, saying unto them all, "I indeed baptize you with water. But one mightier than I cometh, the latchet of whose shoes I am not worthy to unloose. He will baptize you with the Holy Ghost and with fire."

-- Luke 3: 15-16

John never wavered in his belief in the coming of the Christ and the kingdom of God upon the Earth. He died cruelly at the hands of the wicked, but I know that God took him up and exalted him in Heaven. In the flesh, John and Jesus were kindred; in spirit, these kinsmen served only God. John is an inspiration to us because even though he had a high calling, he remained a humble servant of the Lord. This is my goal as a pastor; to humbly serve God in whatever way He calls me. My first calling is to my family; I am a husband to my wife, a father to her children, and I have established a wonderful bond with my own daughter – a true gift from God.

My faith is extremely important to me today, especially in my calling to become a pastor. Since we walk by faith and not by sight, I have an unalterable faith that it was Jesus who changed my heart and my desire for drugs. When I returned to Christ in 1998 I stopped using heroin, but my spirit and soul were just the same, but without dope. Not good enough! I have testified many times to others that it was Jesus who restored my soul and caused my spirit to hunger for more of His infinite love. To be truly "changed," one must want to be more like Christ himself. I think this is especially true for a pastor – one who would lead others to the Lord. When Jesus asked Peter, "Who do you say that I am?" and Peter replied, "You are the Christ, the Son of the living God," Peter was stead-fastly proclaiming his belief in Jesus despite later denying even knowing Him three times. When the hour of his crucifixion arrived, Peter begged to be hung upside down, saying he was unworthy to die as his Lord did. Peter was a true pastor who led his flock until the very Moment of his death. He faltered, as pastors sometimes do being merely human, but his belief and love of Christ sustained him.

As a pastor I know I must remain true to myself and to God. I can never take the credit for my healing from addiction and my compulsion to keep using drugs. ***Recovery from addiction is an "inside" job!*** Without Jesus Christ in my life, neither my body nor my soul would have survived drugs' satanic grasp. If you examine the first three steps of Alcoholics Anonymous, you'll see that we are asked to admit that we are powerless over the drug, that only God can heal us, and that we must accept that healing. The founders of AA, Bill W. and Dr. Bob, got sober (and stayed that way) through a spiritual awakening. I believe that AA was designed by these men to lead others to God, but they leave out the "middle man" – Jesus Christ! This is what I will declare as a pastor, that no one comes to the Father without first believing in His Son. Jesus Himself has said this is so.

My fellowship in recovery comes from others who also have a strong church background. Part of my continuing recovery is through helping parents in our church of addicted children and don't know where to turn; they come to me because they know my story, which is no secret from anyone. I believe that since God doesn't make mistakes, I am right where He wants me to be to do His work. As I grow in his Word, no doubt He will lay straight the path He puts before me. I continue to study the Bible every day and preach sermons at my church. Being the church's youth minister keeps me very busy and fulfilled! My life today revolves around serving God, my family, my church and my friends in Christ. My life has never been fuller!

Friedrich Nietzsche wrote that "He who does not remember the past is condemned to repeat it." I do remember, but I choose not to dwell or brood upon any part of the past. My task as a pastor, husband, father, son, and friend is to ever lead myself and those entrusted to me forward in life. Without this attitude, I would be merely a blind guide.

In 1997 I found out that I had contracted hepatitis C, no doubt due to my use of dirty needles when I was shooting dope. Hepatitis impairs liver function, which is vital to our body's functions. My doctors told me that, against all odds, I had a mild case that needs to be evaluated about once a year. I have no adverse symptoms, but I do need to keep an eye on this condition. Although hepatitis is nothing to take lightly, I recall that I shared needles with other addicts who were HIV-positive or hepatitis-positive and I simply didn't care because the shot was more important than anything else. Today, as I reflect upon my calling to become a pastor, I think that I must be the most blessed man still alive! My faith tells me that God spared me from fatal illnesses that so often afflict addicts so that I could bear witness to His healing power. For me to waste this gift of life is unthinkable. If you enjoy classic literature, you may recall the final words in Herman Melville's *Moby Dick:* "I alone survived to tell thee."

We go forward in the noisy confusion of life not knowing what tasks and troubles may await us in the journey. But let us not be dismayed, for Jesus Christ

– the Alpha and the Omega, the Beginning and the End, the First and the Last – will be with us even until the end of time.

"For unto us a Child is born. Unto us a Son is given. And His name shall be called Wonderful, Counselor, the Mighty God, the Everlasting Father, and the Prince of Peace. King of Kings and Lord of Lords. And He shall reign forever and ever. Hallelujah!

—— From G. F. Handel's *Messiah*
Taken from the Book of Isaiah

CONCLUSION AND ACKNOWLEDGEMENTS

"Perhaps God gave the answers to those who once had nothing to say. But then the years are forgiving; if God's forgiving in kind, perhaps we'll all find our answers somewhere in time." (Savatage – "Streets: A Rock Opera")

God takes what other people mean to be evil and makes it into something positive and beautiful. Everything that happened to me in my life has made me the person that I am today, with both my strengths and shortcomings. I wouldn't trade my life's many learning experiences even if I could have a "do over." When I look back, I still mourn for Anthony. I know that I will see him again in that city not made by hands. How he must smile when I sing in the band at church! Okay, so I'm not a rock star as we once dreamed, but I hope singing in church is as much

> "Lord, take me where You want me to be today, and help me do the things You would have me do. And then, Lord, help me stay out of Your way!"
>
> — Fr. Mychal Judge Head Chaplain, New York City Fire Department. Killed September 11, 2001

of a blessing to others as it is to me. When I look forward, I know that my Redeemer lives, and that I will join Him with Laura in the many mansions of our Father's house which He has prepared for me.

Like everyone, I have my fears and worries. As glorious as my marriage has been, it has seen highs and lows as can be expected in any marriage. Establishing relationships with my step-children has been a challenge not only for me, but for them as well. And my beloved Kaycee is now a teenager. It's been a struggle for us, too. I don't like to say "I'll try." As Jedi Master Yoda said in *Star Wars,* "Do, or do not. There is no "try."

The core of my belief is simple: God gave us a book called the Holy Bible. It contains sixty-six love letters from God to all of us, His most beloved creation. Everything we need to know about life is contained in this book. It holds the answers to all our questions, the solutions to all our problems, the strength to withstand the fallen angel who is the Enemy of God, and the comfort that we seek. The

Bible introduces us to the Lamb of God who took upon himself the sins of the world; by His wounds, we are healed.

This may not have been an easy book for you to read because it vividly describes the world of the drug addict. If you're addicted, you know this book portrays the truth about your world. If you love someone who is addicted, don't let this book dishearten you; pray constantly for your loved one who has lost his or her way. Claim the absolute power of Jesus Christ to defeat the Enemy's snare of addiction. Standing up to the addict and refusing to be his or her enabler is extremely difficult and resolution may not come right away. Remember that when you gaze into the dead, soulless eyes of an addict, you're not looking at your loved one anymore; you are looking into the vicious eyes of Satan. Read your Bible and know that the Lord Jesus Christ will bind Satan and all his works. *Never* is healing too late or salvation denied!

"So after all those one-night stands
Here you are, heart in hand
A child alone
Upon the road
Retreating.
Regretful for the things you're not
And all the dreams you haven't got
Without a home
A heart of stone
Lies bleeding.
For all the roads you followed

**And for all you did not find
For all the things you had to leave behind —**

**I am the way, I am the light
I am the dark inside the night
I hear your hopes
I feel your dreams
And in the dark I hear your screams
Don't turn away, just take my hand
And when you make your final stand
I'll be right there – I'll never leave
All I ask of you is....believe."**

**— Jon Oliva, Chriss Oliva,
and Paul O'Neil of Savatage
"Believe"**

I want to acknowledge and thank the contributors to this book for their inspiration, wisdom and hope. Those individuals whom I've quoted don't even know that they've been major sources of understanding, but I'm sure they would approve, given the circumstances.

First, you'll see that I've quoted heavily from the progressive rock band Savatage and their precedent-setting rock opera, "Streets." In many ways, this story is remarkably similar to events in my own life. In the 1980's, Savatage consisted of Jon Oliva, Chriss Oliva, Steve "Doc" Wacholz, and Johnny Lee Middleton. Lyricist Paul O'Neil was an invaluable part of the group. After Chriss Oliva was killed by a drunk driver in 1992, his brother Jon disbanded

Savatage and it gradually morphed into today's fabulous Trans-Siberian Orchestra. I would be remiss without giving Savatage their "propers" for "Streets:"

All songs written by Jon Oliva, Chriss Oliva
and Paul O'Neil
Copyright 1991
Based on a book written by Paul O'Neil
All lyrics copyright 1991

In the 1980's, Ozzy Osbourne and his guitarist (now deceased) Randy Rhodes literally invented the music genre of "heavy metal." The music world is well familiar with Ozzy's life-long struggle with drugs, alcohol and mental illness. Many of his songs reflect this struggle which today, at age 59, he has finally won. Ozzy is an intelligent and intensely spiritual man, and his later music displays this side of his complex personality.

Zakk Wylde is arguably the best heavy metal guitarist in the world today. In addition to playing with Ozzy Osbourne's band, Zakk also leads the Black Label Society as lyricist and on lead guitar. A life-long Christian, Zakk never fails to pray before he performs and proclaims his priorities in life to be God and his family.

Thanks also to singer/songwriters Billy Joel and John Kay of Steppenwolf for telling the truth about the effects of heroin addiction.

I have quoted liberally everything from the Holy Bible, to Dante's *Inferno*, to William Shakespeare and more. From this eclectic collection of wisdom, I hope you have gained the same inspiration as I have.

Since this book is the true story of my life, I think it best to give Mark Twain the last word:

> **Truth is stranger than fiction because fiction has to make sense.**